♥ Wendy Negley

poems

The heart has no rules.

BANYAN · TREE · PRESS

The Heart Has No Rules

Copyright © 2021 Wendy Negley. All Rights Reserved.

No part of this book may be reproduced or transmitted
in any form or by any means electronic or mechanical including photocopying, recording, or by any information storage and retrieval system without written permission from the copyright holder.

ISBN: 978-1-948261-46-3
Library of Congress Control Number: 2021922557

Interior Design: Christa Mella
Cover & Interior Design: Diane Woods

Published 2021 by Banyan Tree Press,
an imprint of Hugo House Publishers, Ltd.
Denver Colorado, Austin Texas.

DEDICATION

To my mother and my sister
who would have loved these
poems.

CONTENTS

Introduction	9
Love Moves to Rage	13
I Fell In Love with the You-ness of You	14
Playing with Fire	15
Love in A Pandemic	17
Yesterday, Today, Tomorrow	18
A Certain Face	19
Think of my love	22
Between us there are moments	24
Sand and stone and	25
There's no more floating	26
My Grandmother's Eyes	29
For My Sister Who Wanted Me to Write Her a Poem Before, Not After, She Died	30
The Heart Has No Rules	32
He Came	33
A Poem for my Sister, Dying of Cancer	34
For Rhonda	36
When the Music Stops, Before the Dance Begins	37
For Ted	38
The Kiss	39
Reading Between the Lines	40
His Song	41
Now's the longest night of the year	42
Changed My Mind	43

Waiting	44
Days	45
Once in a Blue Moon	46
An Odd Way of Courting	47
Time is a Liar	48
Life and Death Walk Hand in Glove	49
The Room	50
Flying to You	51
Truth at 5 A.M.	52
Three Words	54
Secret	55
Still Waiting	56
Leaving Las Vegas	58
The Story of Us	60
Silly for Billy	61
Grandmother In Love	62
Love	63
I Always Thought Life	65
The Power of Love	66
Love is not Blind	67
For Dennis in his Next Life	68
Asleep I hear a call	70
The Dying Leave Us	72
The Call	73
A Dream	75
You	76
Control-S	77

The Poet	78
The Trouble Today or the Cowboy's Lament	79
I Was Really a Cowgirl at Heart	80
Girl From Little Rock	81
They Say	82
The Portal	84
Sometimes 2	86
Love is Funny	87
Coming to my Senses	88
This Body	90
You Hold my Heart	92
Ridiculous	93
Love for Now	95
On Choosing Music for the Wedding	97
A Wedding	98
A Second-Hand Wife	101
It's You	102
A Poem	105
Dreamer	106
A New Day	108
An Uprising in my Mind	110
They Write Themselves	111
He Said She Said	112
Welcome Home	113
Because Love Is	115
About Wendy	117

INTRODUCTION

These poems have been written over many years with two of them as early as 1965. They mainly deal with love and death and those elements of the human experience which called for a sublimation into meaning and aesthetics. They are offered in the hope that others will find some recognitiion of their own experiences and feel those experiences have been made more beautiful or meaningful herewith.

We are all understanding and so we seek to understand others, the world and ourselves. Poetry helps to elevate our attempts at understanding into art.

I hope these poems help you to do that for yourself.

poems

The heart has no rules.

 Wendy Negley

LOVE MOVES TO RAGE

Love moves to rage

Through glooms of stone

Through dooms of bone

Youth comes to age

Through fresh of green

Through flesh of seen

Door comes to cage

Through sight of blind

Through light of mind

Word comes to page.

I FELL IN LOVE WITH THE YOU-NESS OF YOU

I fell in love with the you-ness of you

The essence of being I saw to be true

But I was stuck in the then-ness of then

I prayed and I hoped that we'd have a when

And here I am set in the now-ness of now

With your hand in mine beside me somehow

The you and the then and the when and the now

Have all joined together and hit me ka-pow!

And when we are ever and now is a then

I'll still love you over and over again.

PLAYING WITH FIRE

All children learn:
You play with fire
You get burned.

All lovers learn:
A flame that's hot
Can also burn.

We lit a torch
That seared my soul,
I knew I'd never
Get out whole.

Then from the ashes
Rose anew
The love I'd always
Had for you.

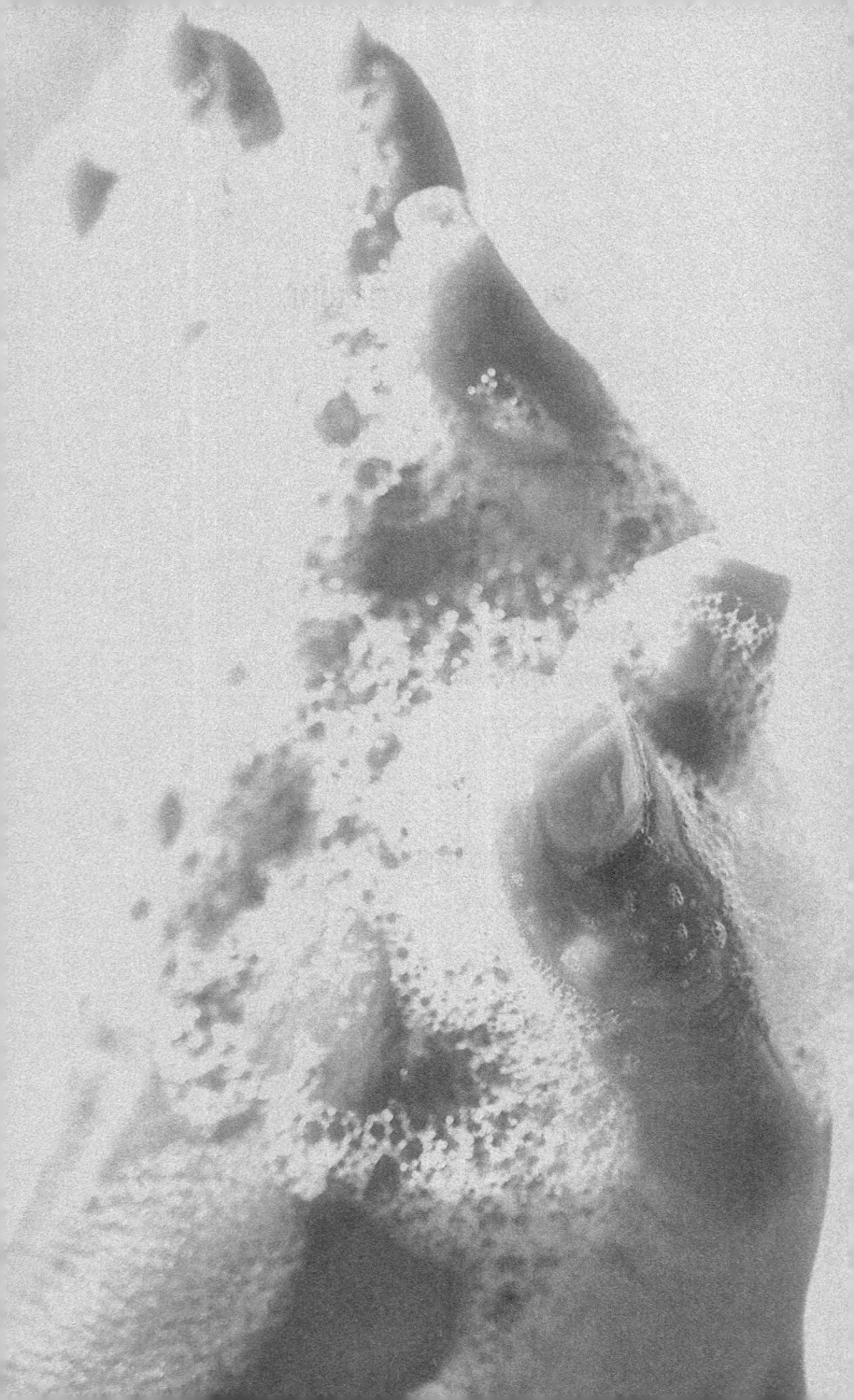

LOVE IN A PANDEMIC

Here I am as I've been told

Sheltered from the rain and cold

I wash my hands with lots of soap

I'm doing all I can to cope

My thoughts however, are of you

Are you safe where you are too?

I disinfect my house again

And worry if you are in pain

The distance makes it all seem worse

Imagination's been a curse

You must forgive my frequent call

For you must know you are my all.

YESTERDAY, TODAY, TOMORROW

Yesterday, today,

Tomorrow

Are just time.

My love is yours and

Yours is mine.

That is a truth

We find sublime.

A CERTAIN FACE

a time

a place

a certain face

will fade

with the last ray of sun

but love

lives on

love breathes

without air

love flows

without water

love speaks

without sound

love moves

without motion

the time

the place

that certain face

are gone

the love

lives on

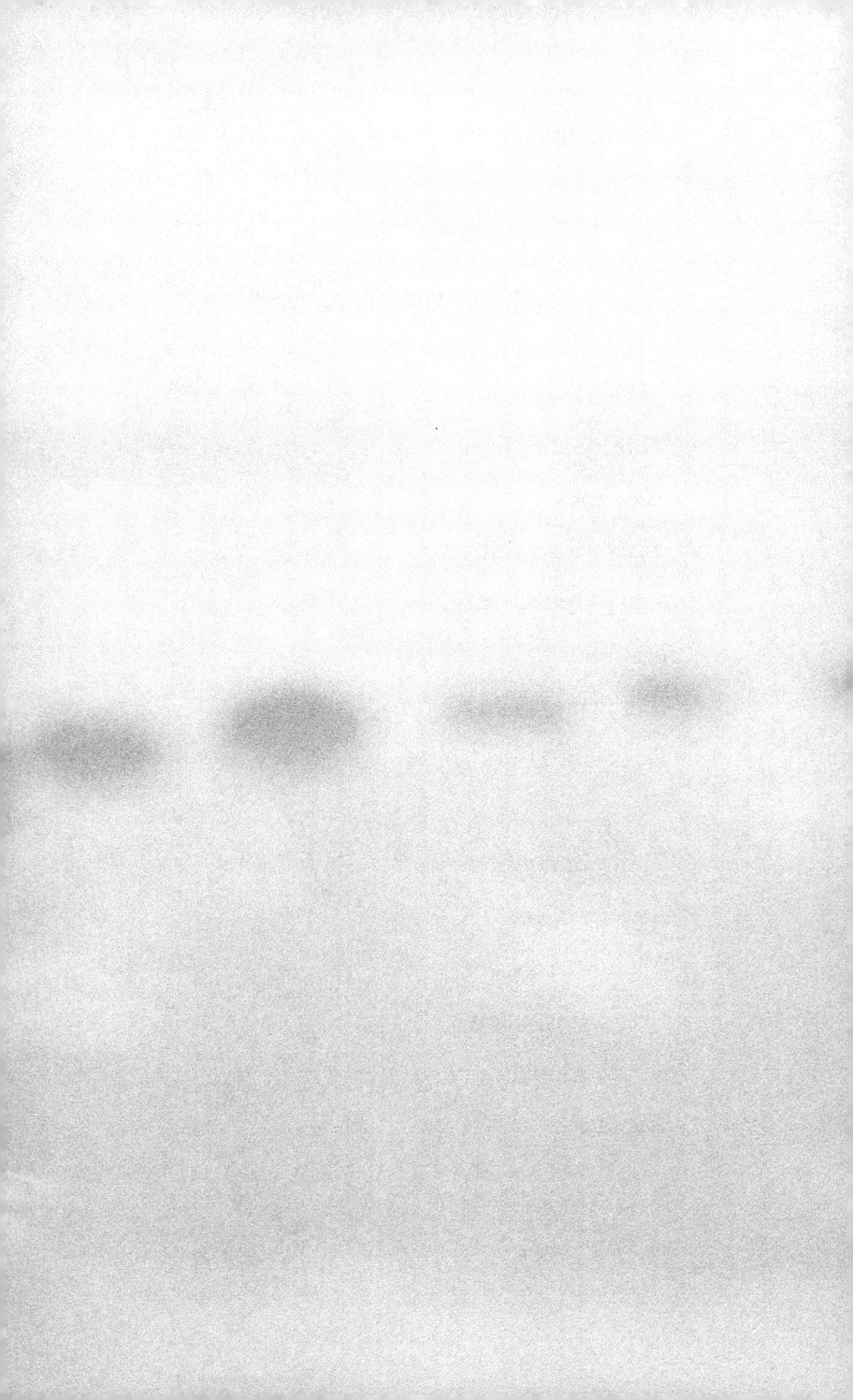

THINK OF MY LOVE

Think of my love
As a rock:
You can hold it,
It is palpable, real
Not illusive,
It is firmly there
Not rare.

Think of my love
As a pebble:
It is ordinary
Every day, known
Not extraordinary
Not alone.

Think of my love

As a pathway:

It is well tended,

It goes somewhere,

It is familiar

To your footsteps.

BETWEEN US THERE ARE MOMENTS

Between us there are moments

When there is no between

I carry them with me

Like soft smooth stones taken home

From the beach in my palm

To touch now and now and again now

When you, like the ocean, are far

Away, and I am busy

With thoughts and bread.

The warmth in my hand

Flows through me

Filling the room

The waves roll in.

SAND AND STONE AND

Sand and stone and

sand and stone and water

carved and crumbled

counting the time without number

held in the hand for the calm

soaked in the skin of its hunger

rolled in the bed where it tumbled

held in the palm a bit longer

sand and stone and

sand and stone and water

THERE'S NO MORE FLOATING

There's no more floating
in the river now
now that the dam gave out
and all the water came over the rocks
water came screaming over the rocks
"Dave did it" Charley said
and gave him the general blame
though we all had taken some little rock
or maybe a twig here or there
or watched and said nothing
till David pulled the last one out
and the well contained water
roared down with a shout
now the water won't hold you
up anymore
since the dam came
raging down.

MY GRANDMOTHER'S EYES

My grandmother's eyes

In the old school photos

So solemn

From hard work and sorrow.

My grandmother's eyes

In a moment of love,

So soft,

Unaccustomed to softness.

My grandmother's eyes

In my own daughter's face,

So eager,

My grandmother's eyes

live forever.

FOR MY SISTER, WHO WANTED ME TO WRITE HER A POEM BEFORE, NOT AFTER, SHE DIED

So, look, I said,

it's easy writing a poem

for the dead.

They don't complain

or take offense

but just accept

whatever I may write

without a fight.

But

to write a poem for one

who's filled with life

and love

and fifty million

thoughts a sec…

aw heck!

THE HEART HAS NO RULES

The heart has no rules or bounds

The mind is busy on its rounds

It's always coming up with reasons

It never stops for any seasons

The heart aches

The heart breaks

It never asks for why or how

It keeps on loving now and now

The heart continues on and on

The mind is meaning

The heart is song.

HE CAME

He came
It will ever be
A thrill to me
To see
Him at my door
He came
No waiting
Any more
He came
So sweet
A sight
For that
I might give up
Everything
He came
Now my heart
Can sing

A POEM FOR MY SISTER DYING OF CANCER

She was a lady

(no, scratch that, too sexist, she wouldn't like that)

She was a woman

(no, still sexist, if I was writing this for a man would I bother to state his gender?)

(actually, I probably would because I have to call him something)

(start over)

She was a person

(forget it, just write from the heart)

If one could have two hearts,

She was my other heart.

The one that always told me where home is.

Rhonda,

You'll always

Be home

In my heart.

FOR RHONDA

The sky is gray
birds sing anyway
gray is the color of my mind
suspended here
beside you
waiting
for death to arrive
and take you.
Death is black
but here it is all gray
birds sing anyway

WHEN THE MUSIC STOPS. BEFORE THE DANCE BEGINS

When the music stops
Before the dance begins,
When the motion dies
Before the death of the lover:
You stand at the edge
And the silence around you
Pushes you over.

Then you enter the fog.

To survive the fog
And the falling,
To feel it condense
And the landing
To be cold and wet
But still standing
Is to go beyond.

Now the dance begins.

FOR TED

your love, this air I breathe and walk through,

movement into movement, fluidly

surrounds me not enclosing but

opening forever

my love, this earth you live and walk on

moment into moment, its mountains

rivers, valleys, birds and flowers open

and enclose you, singing, curved beneath the curved space of

this air, your love.

THE KISS

You kissed me
Unexpected
Unrequested
Unsuggested
But…
Uncontested
Just a kiss
A tiny touch
Sending ripples
To the shore
Becoming waves
Of something more
You kissed me
A tidal wave
Engulfed me
Ever more.

READING BETWEEN THE LINES

Between us things cannot be said
What still we must impart
With care you tell me your designs
And I must listen with my heart
And learn to read between the lines.

Now all my hopes and dreams are based
Upon a shaky ground
I hear your words and how they sound
But I must listen with my heart
And there the meaning can be found

Perhaps one day we'll be allowed
To speak with open truth
Till then we tiptoe round the mines
And we must listen with the heart
And learn to read between the lines.

HIS SONG

"You've got me on a string
It's just a potent thing
You come into the room
My heart goes bop-a-boom
Before I can decide
I'm right by your side
You are my puppeteer
Whenever you are near
You've got me on a string
It's just a potent thing."

That was years ago, he said.
You'd think that it would all be dead.
And yet, you called, I came
Could I still feel the same?
You've got me on a string
It's still a potent thing.

NOW'S THE LONGEST NIGHT OF THE YEAR

Now is the longest night of the year

It will be long for you're not here

I yearn to say what I would do

If I could spend this night with you

And are you thinking of me, too?

Oh my, the things that we could do!

I WENT AND CHANGED MY MIND

I went and changed my mind

But, yet, I feared that I might find

I had upset some part of your design

You have no right to say

Just how I ought to spend my day

I have no right to seek

The wishes that you cannot speak

And so, life goes around

And I must stand on my own ground

And hope I do not break

The future that I wish to make.

WAITING

"I live each day
Much like the last
I wake
I eat
I brush my teeth
I take the bus
I work
I take the bus
I eat
I sleep
I wake
Repeat
I talk
I laugh
I see my friends
And no one knows
I'm waiting
I'm waiting for you
I'm waiting for me
I'm waiting for a time
When we can be
I sleep
I wake
I wait

DAYS

Sixty days
Stretch like stones
That I must pass
To reach you.
Oh, I will cross
But I must clamp
A hold upon my soul
That I not fall
Or slip to doubt
Or ruin all.
I am so close
To heart's desire
I would not fall into the mire
Or have it all go up in fire
So I will walk with certain grace
And smile again to see your face.
In days
Sixty days.

ONCE IN A BLUE MOON

Once in a blue moon
I find myself
Here with you
Once in a blue moon
It's rare they say
Yet here we two
We have our day
You never know
How life will turn
So long ago
We could just yearn
Yet here we are
Two as one
Tomorrow will see
Another sun
Another day
We travel on
 The open way
But we travel
Hand in hand
And as we leave
Blue moon behind
We have in truth
What once was
A glimmer in our mind.

AN ODD WAY OF COURTING

You have an odd way of courting me
Not the way it's supposed to be
A catalog of your faults and flaws
Is it meant to give me pause?
You never say you love me
You don't laud my beauty
You say you'll make me breakfast
For the rest of my life
You don't propose but you do say
You want me for your wife
You want to drive me to and from work
You want to take care of my every quirk
Now what is my reply?
What do I say to this funny guy?
You know, I need a man.
I say,
To make me breakfast
Every day.

TIME IS A LIAR

Time is a liar
It says that we must always change
It tells us that we have reached an age
It takes our ownership away
It makes us think we cannot play
Time is a liar
It would have us all believe
In loss for which we have to grieve
It would have us stuck in stone
Thinking that we must atone
Time is a liar
And here we live within its spell
From morning sun to dinner bell
Oh, it has chained us good and well
So much we cannot even tell
Time is a liar
I don't know how to break its bond
Except to know I go beyond
And some day soon I will be gone
To freely go for what I long
Time is a liar

We are truth

LIFE AND DEATH WALK HAND IN GLOVE

Life and Death walk hand in glove

Though Life for Death can show no love

Death worships Life and longs to hold her

But she, of course, ignores his ardor

Life sings and laughs and dances

Death isn't taking any chances

Life laughs at Death and runs away

Death knows some time he'll have his day

That final day Life breathes her last

She finds that Death holds her hand fast

She smiles at her truest friend

At last together at the end.

THE ROOM

The door said start
The wall said halt
The floor was rocking
With a jolt.

The door said go
The wall said no
The floor was singing
Do si do.

I said, "Room you've gone too far
You don't remember what you are."

I nailed a picture on the wall
I swept the floor into the hall
And on the door I wrote my name.

That room's been quiet
Since I came.

FLYING TO YOU

It's a long flight

We are steadily making our way

Above the clouds

I can't see the land below

Hidden from view

But still I know we are

Coming home to you

Just so my life

Has been a journey

The pathway hidden

But steady motion

That ends at last

In reunion with you.

TRUTH AT 5 A.M.

Sometimes it works

Sometimes it hurts

Sometimes it doesn't make sense

Sometimes you've won

Sometimes you're done

Sometimes it's not worth a pence

Sometimes he's true

Sometimes you're blue

Sometimes you're out in the rain

Sometimes you're lost

Sometimes you're boss

Sometimes are not worth the pain

Sometimes you can't sleep

Sometimes you can't weep

Sometimes you just stay in bed

Sometimes you can feel

Sometimes you can heal

Sometimes it's all in your head

But then there are times

When everything rhymes

And everything turns into song

And sometimes are okay

Because there's that day

You finally know you belong

Right here by your side

That's where I'll abide

Through all the times short or long.

THREE WORDS

Three words

I never thought you'd say

Three words

That blew my doubts away

Three words

That warmed my soul

Three words

That made me whole.

SECRET

I think I didn't even know

How much I love you

It had to be a secret

I kept it tight

I didn't even let myself in

I just waited

Not knowing quite

For what I longed

Now the word is out

And I find you are

My heart's only song.

STILL WAITING

Space is my

Enemy

Time is my

Friend

To traverse

Both

Must be my

End

One million

Seconds

More or less

Until we have our

Next caress

The earth must travel neath

The sun

A dozen times

Until we're done

With waiting.

Oh Lord

Let me be done

With waiting.

LEAVING LAS VEGAS

The plane takes off and

Leaves the ground

Vegas growing small

Makes no sound

Where it was loud and

Bright last night

All drums and

Glaring neon light.

Here in the capital of sin

Our virtue was applauded

Here in the land of hope to win

Our jackpot was awarded.

What Vegas doesn't dare to hype

Is the truth of love

And living right.

Below me Vegas

Falls behind

People come in

 Hopes to find

Whatever dreams

They have in mind.

My dream came true

Because of you

For that I'll give

Las Vegas her due.

THE STORY OF US

We met
We talked
We laughed
We kissed
We had to part
We missed
We yearned
We loved and learned
As years went by
A loss occurred
It meant we could retry
We met
We talked
We laughed
We kissed
Together now
We live
We love
We're one
We have begun

SILLY FOR BILLY

I don't know what's come over me
I just keep writing poetry
I'm higher than a flag in June
I'm singing every funny tune
I'm listening to the buzz of bees
I'm trading secrets with the trees
I've gone so high I can't come down
I'm flying over every town
My ship has come to every port
My men have conquered every fort
I'm dancing tangos with the Stars
I'm buying rounds in all the bars
I'm laughing as I write this verse
I don't know how it could get worse
You tell me that I should be grave
But life worth living's all I crave
You ask me what has set me free
It's just because he now loves me!

GRANDMOTHER IN LOVE

(Apologies to Lewis Carroll*)

You're old Grandmother, the young girl said
And yet you can take a new man to your bed?
I think that you must have gone out of your head.

My hair may be silver and my mind may be slow
But the young girl inside me can still feel that glow
My love is as strong as it was long ago

I'm not a grandmother who knits by the fire
I'm just a woman who calls time a liar
And loves who I want with all my desire

So look at me clearly and see who I am
And know that your life is yours to command
And shouldn'ts and shoulds are not worth a damn!

*Reference to the poem "You are Old Father William" in Lewis Carroll's, The Adventures of Alice in Wonderland.

LOVE

Love
Is not Fate's Ferris Wheel which
takes you up then turns Its back
and you come down.

Love
Is not Sex's Roller Coaster
That takes you for a fast free ride
Then drops you off at home
Alone

Love
Is the little Carousel
In the corner, worn old
With steady turning
And Love
Has its own music
Playing in the center

> ("You see what I mean?"
> Said the ticket man
> "It doesn't start, it doesn't
> End, It just goes round
> No up and down."

"So does the Earth. So what?"
You said putting your
Money down.

He winked. He whispered.
"See that ring? You get it
And you win the prize."

"What's the prize?"
I said wide-eyed.

He shrugged.
"You win and you decide.")

Love
Goes round and we
Ride waiting.

Quick
See there's the ring.
We reach.

Love
Goes round and we ride
Reaching.

I ALWAYS THOUGHT LIFE

I always thought life
Should be lived in song
In times of feeling
A tune would give tongue
Better than words or tears
Or an angry shout
To that which our heart
Is really about.
Like we're in
A Lerner and Loewe
Or Rogers and Hammerstein
Musical show.
Like Disney always
Showed us to do
Let's sing any time
A feeling comes through.
And when you're in love
That sweet harmony
Is what you'll be singing
Your true melody.

THE POWER OF LOVE

I put your picture by my bed

I see it when I turn my head

I feel a smile bloom on my face

Just to see you in my space

Where once there was a lonely heart

Now love says that we'll never part

This is the power that love can give

It makes us know that we can live

Now I'm grinning ear to ear

Just to see your picture here!

LOVE IS NOT BLIND

They say that love is blind
But love has been maligned
Love doesn't see with eyes
Love is much more wise
Love sees deep and true
A love-only view
Of the naked heart
Seen without art
Of the simple soul
Seen clear as a whole
Love can take a chance
Mixing in romance
An eyes wide open view
And all that's seen is you.

FOR DENNIS IN HIS NEXT LIFE

Midnight and a baby cries

He dreams of loved ones that he knew

Their whispers and their sighs

Out of reach and fading fast

The voices of his past

He dreams of one who was his wife

He loved her in that other life

And of his children now all grown

Who had children of their own

He cries that he must start anew

And relearn all that he once knew

When just anon he was a man

He feels this wasn't in his plan

His parents come to give him aid

And wonder at his small tirade

Their love will comfort to him give

And he'll decide that he can live

That last life will fade away

And he can live another day

And he can go another way

ASLEEP I HEAR A CALL

Asleep I hear a call
"Where are you?"
Your voice as you used to ask
I'm here but the question is
Where are YOU?
I know I didn't hear
The sound waves of your voice
Just a dream or memory
Of how it used to be
Across the chasm
That is death,
Are you calling me?
Our bodies are forever
Cast aside
Our love forever is
Together tied
Do you miss me in the
Place where you now lie?
I rise from bed and
Start my day

As this is still my life.

THE DYING LEAVE US

The dying leave us

Such a mess

There's never

A return address

I'd love to send them

Each a card

"Without you, Darling,

Life is hard!"

THE CALL

Wendy!

I heard the call

It came through well

Despite the wall

I looked around

No one was seen

You are gone

What does this mean?

Do you desire

To be with me

Despite the change

In your identity?

Love knows no death

It knows no time

But I'm still here

This life still mine

I don't know how

To answer you

Or how to reach

Beyond the blue

I hope that you

Can settle in

To the new life

That you begin

Perhaps we'll meet

A future year

My love for you

Will still be clear.

A DREAM

"What are you doing here?

You know you've been dead

For almost a year."

He turned and smiled

As I'd not seen in awhile

"I'm getting married again you know"

His smile just continued to grow

Morning came and I was alone

Wond'ring just what I had been shown

I know that you loved me

And that you still do

It seems that you're happy

So I'm happy too.

YOU

You, the word I write so much,
Your laugh your smile your touch
You wish perhaps I wouldn't say
So much that gives our love away
I could write it as a curse
Make your actions look their worse
Make you bow your head in shame
Make you want to change your name
But you know that I wouldn't do
Because it just would not be true
You, my Dear, must bear the stress
Of having the love of a poetess.

CONTROL-S

Once again the poem came
When I was outside the frame
I had to do the task at hand
Before I met the mind's demand
If control-S was in the mind
All those lines again I'd find
Instead I must create anew
Just to say these thoughts to you.
I don't know if the words I wrote
Are quite as good as those I thought
But here it is in black and white
Preserved against the coming light
The thoughts all vanish as they come
The poem will live past the dawn.

THE TROUBLE TODAY OR THE COWBOY'S LAMENT

The trouble today

is quite simply that

The bad guys don't always

wear a black hat.

The good guys don't always

dress all in white

How do I know which one

I should fight?

THE POET

A specialized insanity

Uniquely fitted just to me

Yet known to poets for all time

And to songwriters versed in rhyme

My heart is pounding in my head

To make my feelings better said

To put these words upon the page

That tumble out as in a rage

I need to voice my love for you

I need to say it swift and true

So for all time it's plain to see

That you're the one who undoes me.

I WAS ALWAYS REALLY A COWGIRL AT HEART

I was always really a cowgirl at heart

A do it or die kind of girl

A let's take it all not just a part

Ready to give it a whirl

I want a guy who's really a man

Who can take what comes at him

And give me a hand

In handling my life

The best that I can

I don't want a dream or a wish anymore

I want muscle and bone to come to my door

Your wrinkles and warts are beauty to me

I always say I see what I see

And you are the one I want by my side

So don't stand there waiting

Get ready to ride!

GIRL FROM LITTLE ROCK

Not bad for a girl from Arkansas
That's what they might say
As they view me with awe
Oh, I'm not any kind of
Celebrity
No one will watch me
Live on TV
I'm just a girl
Who does what she can
To learn about people
So I understand
And use what I know
To give them a hand.
That's pretty good
For a girl from the block
Who comes from a place
They call Little Rock.

THEY SAY

They say

I should

They say

I must

They say

They know

And I

Should trust

They tell me

What to do or be

And that I

Should just agree

But I can see

A crack or two

And don't think that

I want to do

All that they say

Is best for me

That's just not my

Cup of tea

So I will look and

I will find

And I will make up

My own mind

My lips may smile

Silently

But have no doubt

My thoughts are free.

THE PORTAL

Men and women come
From different planets
You say
And mine is in a galaxy
Far far away.
I hear you talking
Loud and clear
You say there's no
Agreement here
But I've read the books
I know the score
I know somewhere
There is a door
A portal cross that
Deep divide
A door to lead me
To your side
Old magic says
The keys are three
If I can find them all
I'll be

Across that space
And next to thee
The first I find
Is willingness
I must agree with
More or less
Whatever you might
Do or be
It has to be okay
With me
The next is love
And that I share
A vast abundance
Always there
The third and most
Important thing
Communication
That I bring
With it the walls
Will all dissolve
With it alone our
Troubles solve
I have the keys
I'm at the door
Will you meet me
Forever more?

SOMETIMES 2

Sometimes fairy tales are real

Sometimes the truth is how you feel

The ogres vanquished not by sword

The witch is felled by just a word

True love's kiss has won again

The old song with a new refrain

I slept and dreamt my prince would come

I wake and find I'm not alone

You say that you are just a guy

And I should not expect the sky

The tales don't say what "ever after" means

Real life is better than the dreams.

LOVE IS FUNNY

Love is funny

Not always sunny

Can't tear it or crush it

Can't hurry or rush it

It grows at its pace

It won't keep its place

You can nurture and tend it

You can try to upend it

It stays in your heart

It won't come apart

Though some think its dead

They've misplaced it instead

Its under the coals

Alive in their souls

Love is not down

Its always around.

COMING TO MY SENSES

They say I should come to my senses, it seems

I am out of control and giddy with dreams

All I can say in defense is, you see,

My senses have actually all come to me.

My sense of smell finds your scent on my bed

And gives me a picture of you in my head

My sense of touch feels your skin and your hair

Letting me know how much you are there

My sense of taste comes in when we kiss

A taste that can only fill me with bliss

My hearing gives me the sound of your voice

A sound that for me is always first choice

And sight, of course, darling, gives me a view

Of all that is different and worthy in you.

Now I can tell them without any doubt

My senses are all you and I are about!

THIS BODY

I WAS MADE FOR COMFORT NOT FOR SPEED. -- MUDDY WATERS

This body was made for a man

Made for his hand to adore

Made for his mouth to explore

Made for his tongue and his teeth and his lips

From the ends of my toes to my last fingertips

Made for his head to pillow at last

Made for his arms (oh his arms!) to hold fast

Made to ride in a windstorm of passion

And drown in a tidal wave of sensation

It wasn't made for the catwalk of fashion

I won't be found in a designer's collection

No one would call it a thing of perfection

But it's here for you

And hopes you can see

Just what a dream

This body and me.

YOU HOLD MY HEART

You hold my heart

In a place

Where there is neither

Time nor Space

Held as lightly

As a feather

Yet never was so

Firm a tether

It's settled in

To safely weather

All that we must

Face together

You hold my heart

As yours hold I

We breathe as one

Beneath the sky.

RIDICULOUS

Ridiculous of me

To think that we could be

Together

Despite all the miles

And the years

Despite all the qualms

And the fears

Ridiculous of me

To think that if we were

Together

We would be doing all

Of our best

We would be showing all

Of the rest

Together

Here is the way that you

Can live too

Here is the way that you

Can be true

Together

Sometimes as you see

Ridiculous can be

More true

Than expected or normal

Or "Now I must do,"

Thus, we are forever

Together.

LOVE FOR NOW

Always and forever

Are more than I view

I can see now

Is all me and you

Now becomes then

And a new now appears

And now becomes now

And turns into years

I love you now and

Each now as it turns

In each now anew

The flame of love burns

I can't say always

I know not where that ends

I can't say forever

Or what that portends

But I can say now

And that is a flow

A flow that continues

As long as we know.

ON CHOOSING MUSIC FOR THE WEDDING

It must be beautiful you see

But not so much to outshine me

It must speak of my heart

And make our love a thing of art

But not reveal a truth so deep

That any secret we can't keep

Meaning to us both should be

But not for everyone to see

Oh! And I must move along

Feeling like I float in song

And everyone should watch and say

Oh how she glows on this her day!

A WEDDING

A handsome man

In a suit and a vest

A beautiful bride

In a white silk dress

A holy man

With a sacred book

A vow

A vow

I do

I do

A kiss

And thus is born

A life of bliss

A me

A me

Become a

We

Two hearts

Two lives

Meld into

One

A richer life

Has now

Begun.

A SECOND-HAND WIFE

You know I will be
Your second-hand wife
But we needn't live
A second-hand life
Always the past
Is built on anew
An old step is used to
Get a good view
Our lives and our loves
Will add to the mix
We'll be two old dogs who
Can learn new tricks
We're shabby and chic and
Vintage as well
And from all our days we've
Tales to tell
Yet still we'll create a
Life that is new
Your second-hand wife who's
Newly with you.

IT'S YOU

You are my sun

My moon

My heart's lagoon

You fill my day with all its light

You are the wonder of my night

You are the smile across my face

You are the maker of my space

It's you I've wanted for all time

It's you who gives my life its rhyme

A POEM

A poem is not in motion

But it flows

Like liquid down the page

It streams to find

Its place

Among the minds

Of men.

A poem is not ballet

And yet it glides

Across the page

And moves in grace

Not pausing

In one space.

A poem dances in its

Thinking as it

Waltzes in the mind

A poem is not music

But oh my!

It sings.

DREAMER

I'm told that I'm a dreamer

And I suppose I am

But are the dreams a glimmer

Of what's behind the dam?

A dam made up of lies and pain

Of promises denied

And all that must not come again

And all we have decried.

We live now below the dam

Our real selves we have forgot

We live our lives of careful sham

To keep a lid upon our thought

There mustn't be the slightest leak

To tell us what we yet could be

Power sensed at times would speak

Of our innate ability.

The dreamer dreams

The truth of man

The power held back

By the dam

Come dream with me

And let's unleash

The power of truth

That we can reach

A NEW DAY

Sometimes you wake up

In the darkest of night

The black and the sorrow

Fill you with fright

I'm here all alone

In terror you cry

Then pull yourself up

And give this a try

Send every moment

Away and good-by

In just sixty seconds

Each one is the past

More than that moment

Not one will last

So send every moment

To personal hell

Make each new second

Better to dwell

The new day will dawn

Whether we do a thing

But you can determine

Just what it will bring.

The old day is dead

We will miss it not

The new day is here

Let's see what it's brought.

AN UPRISING IN MY MIND

An uprising in my mind

Compelled me out of bed

To write the thoughts

That whirled in my head

The rebels commandeered

My hands

And typed this verse

So all would understand

But, wait! What was it

That I had to say?

Those rebel thoughts

Have all now slipped away

Somewhere there's laughter

At my back

I'm going to bed now

What the heck!

THEY WRITE THEMSELVES

They write themselves

You know

The poems

I just provide the hands

To shape the words

The channel

For the thought

The poems come

And seek to live

I give them

Breath

And form upon

The Earth

They sing

They play

They laugh

As I behold

My work

HE SAID SHE SAID

He said
She said
He said He said
She said She said She said
He said He said He said He said
She said
HesaidHesaidHesaidHesaidHesaidHesaidHESAID
She said She said
HE SAID HE SAID HESAIDHESAID
She said
He said He said
She said

He said

They kissed
She smiled
He smiled

WELCOME HOME

Welcome home, I say
Meaning more than a room and a bed
More than a place to lay down your head
This is a place where you can be free
To be whatever you might care to be
Always a shelter from the storm
Always a place where you will be warm
A base from which you can travel far
A place from which you can follow a star
With never a word of censure or doubt
Never a query of what you're about
A house full of laughter and always of love
A place where there's nothing that you have to prove
And all that is asked is you open your heart
That you enter in and take your full part.
Welcome home, I said,
I've been waiting for you
And all of the wonderful things we can do.

BECAUSE LOVE IS

Because love is
The night is warm
Because love is
No right is wrong
Because love is
The daytime is bright
Because love is
There's always a light
Because love is
We walk hand in hand
Because love is
We do what we can
Because love is
We talk without fear
Because love is
We both will be here
Because love is
The children can sleep
Because love is
No angels will weep
Because love is
We sing the same song
Because love is
We' will always belong
Because love is
Our dreams can come true
Because love is
It will always be you

ABOUT WENDY

She was born Wendy Leigh
Peterson in Chicago, Illinois,
the day after Christmas 1948.
She grew up in Maryland
(where she wrote her first
poem at the age of four),
Alcoa, Tennessee, Little Rock,
Arkansas, and Seattle
Washington. She went to
Antioch College in Ohio and
wrote poetry. She had a
career in education, has been
a spiritual counselor, and
supervisor of spiritual counseling

and served two terms as the Executive Director of a Non-profit organization.
In 1974 she married Dennis Negley and they had two children. In 2015, Dennis and Wendy followed their daughter and grandchildren to Oregon. She continued to be a spiritual counselor in Portland. She wrote poetry. Her husband died in November 2019. She was a widow at 70. In 2020, she was engaged at 71, in 2021, a bride at 72, marrying William Thames

Wendy lives in Beaverton, Oregon with her husband and two cats. The cats belong to her husband but they tolerate her. She would love to hear your thoughts on her poetry. She can be reached at wnegley@gmail.com. Also, see her Facebook page, wendynegleypoet, her Instagram page of the same name and her blog wendynegleypoet.blogspot.com. Website: wendynegleypoet.com

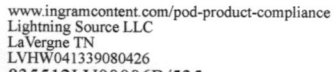
www.ingramcontent.com/pod-product-compliance
Lightning Source LLC
LaVergne TN
LVHW041339080426
835512LV00006B/535